MW00975436

JESUS CHRIST IS LORD

*An Easter Celebration
of Worship and Praise*

Marty Parks

Lillenas PUBLISHING COMPANY

Kansas City, MO 64141

CONTENTS

Jesus Christ Is Lord

Words and Music by
MARTY PARKS
Arranged by Marty Parks

*NARRATOR: Listen! The echo of a timeless theme is heard throughout all the earth. Before anything was created and to this very day, you can hear it. In simple gatherings and in grand

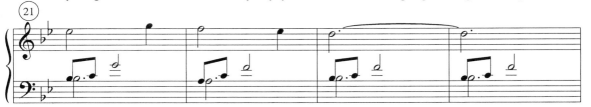

6
6

cathedrals, the majestic hymn of angels and millions of blood-bought saints resounds with this unshakable statement of faith: Jesus Christ is Lord!

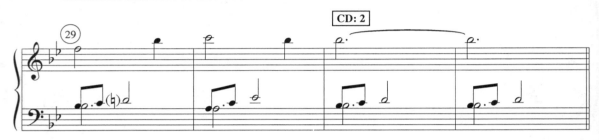

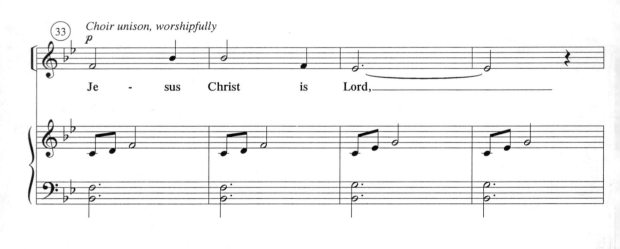

Choir unison, worshipfully

Je - sus Christ is Lord,

Je - sus Christ is Lord;

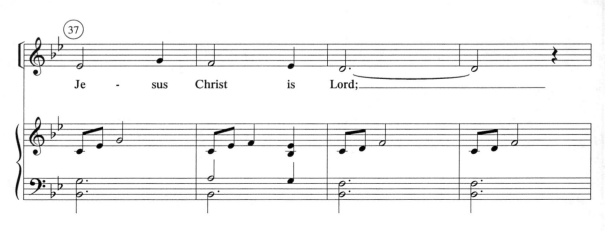

CD: 4

dored: Je - sus Christ is Lord._____

Choir unison

f Je - sus Christ is Lord,_____

Je - sus Christ is Lord;_____

S.A.T.B.

Je - sus Christ is Lord of all,

CD: 5

Je - sus Christ is Lord._____

9

Lord of All

Words and Music by
MARTY PARKS
Arranged by Marty Parks

Brightly ♩ = ca. 98

1st time: Choir unison
2nd time: 2 parts

Lord of all, Je-sus, You're the Lord of all; From the Fa-ther's

own right hand, Still You stand as Lord of all.

Ladies divisi

Lamb of God, Je-sus, You're the Lamb of God;

Men unison

12

Bear-ing all my sin and shame, You be-came the Lamb of God.

Choir unison

Righ - teous, Ho - ly, wor-thy of praise;

Glo - rious Sav - ior, An-cient of Days. Blest Re-deem - er,

CD: 11

might-y to save— Raised in vic - t'ry, con-qu'ring the grave!

2-part

Ris - en King, Je-sus, You're my ris - en King; Now and for e -

For You– For Me

Underscore

MARTY PARKS

NARRATOR *(without music)*: Jesus Christ is Lord! No greater declaration has ever been heard. To a world desperately seeking answers and frantically searching for truth, we have this message: Jesus Christ is Lord. *(music begins)*

CD: 13   Reflectively ♩ = ca. 64

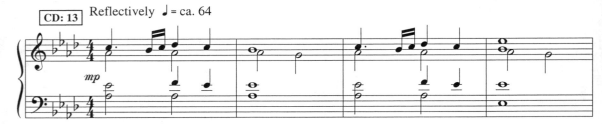

Early Christians greeted one another with these words, for the atoning death of Jesus and His triumphant resurrection were their cause for celebration and the central theme of their

life. And still today, Christ's victory over the grave offers the promise of eternal life for all who call on Him.

Long ago the plan was formed. Jesus, God's Son, would become a man. He would suffer and die for our sins, then rise victorious and ascend to His Father's throne. He is there even now, speaking on our behalf; interceding to the Father for you– for me.

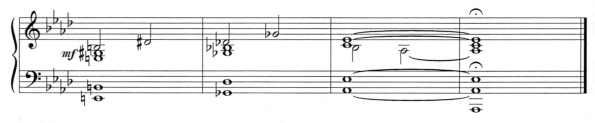

And He's Ever Interceding

Words and Music by
CAROLYN GILLMAN
Arranged by Marty Parks

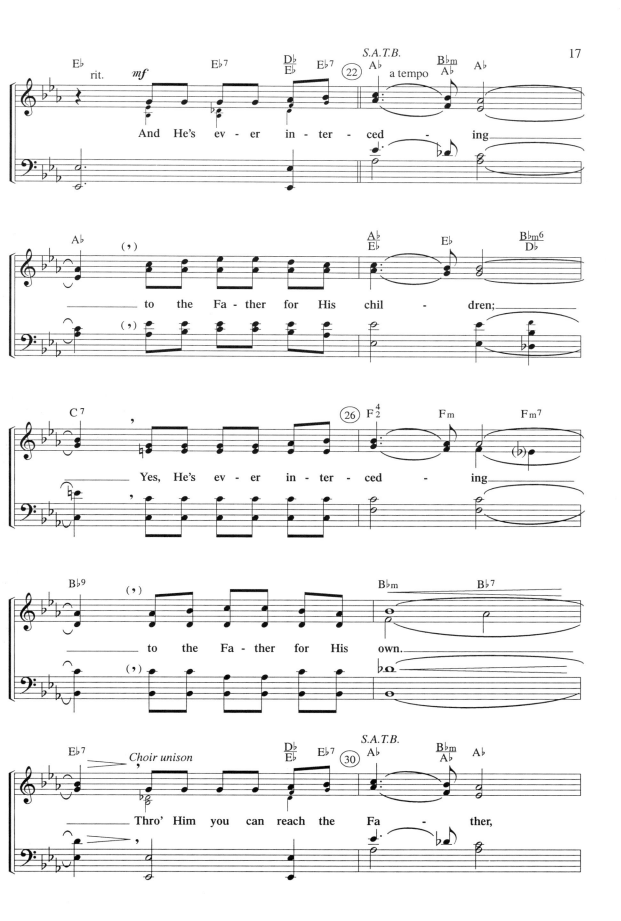

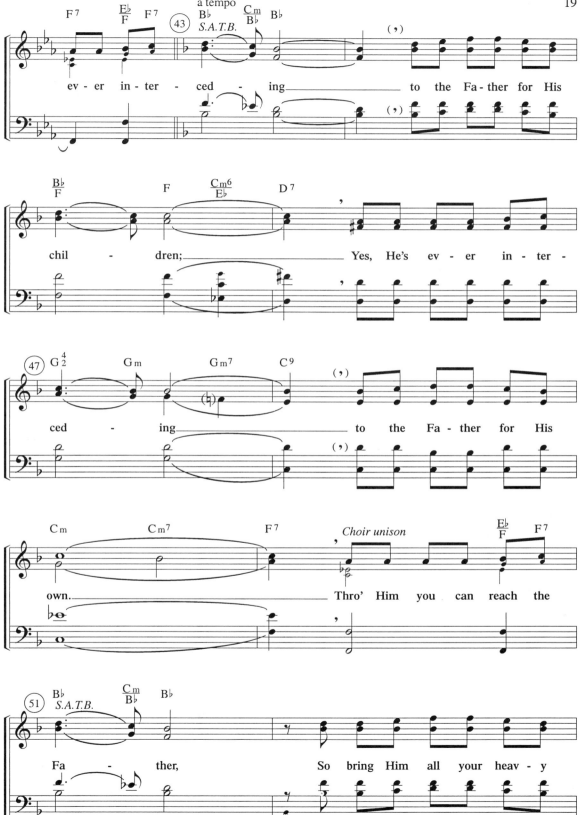

The Sacrifice

Underscore

MARTY PARKS

Simply ♩ = ca. 68

*NARRATOR: This Christ we exalt as Lord has bridged the gap between a holy God and a sinful human race. For centuries, spotless lambs had been offered as atoning sacrifices for

the sins of the people of God. These, however, were merely symbols of the one, perfect Lamb who would cleanse us by His blood.

God's Word tells us that only through the shedding of blood is there forgivness of sins. So, Jesus, the Lamb, became our sacrifice.

He Has Surely Borne Our Sorrow

with
Written in Red

Words and Music by
MOSIE LISTER
Arranged by Marty Parks
A cappella; keyboards may assist*

*This selection is in the same key as the preceding underscore, so the instrumental introduction here is not absolutely necessary. If needed or desired, however, accompanist may play the printed introduction and derive an accompaniment from the choral parts. Track is provided on companion products.

23

*Words and Music by Gordon Jensen. Copyright © 1984 Word Music, Inc. All rights reserved. Used by permission.

Redeemed

Underscore

MARTY PARKS

NARRATOR: The greatest pain that Jesus suffered was not the pain of nails that pierced His body. His deepest agony was that of sin– our sin; that separation from God that He willingly took upon Himself.

All this happened that we might be redeemed. We've been purchased for God, not with perishable things like silver or gold…but with the precious blood of Christ.

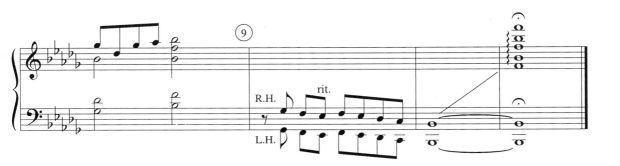

I Will Sing of My Redeemer

with
Redeemed

PHILIP P. BLISS

JAMES MCGRANAHAN
Arranged by Marty Parks

Solo: medium voice

1. I___ will sing_____ of my___ Re-
(2. I___ will) tell_____ the won - drous

28

I Will Praise Him

with

It Is Well with My Soul

Words and Music by
MARGARET J. HARRIS
Arranged by Marty Parks

32

34

The Third Day

Underscore

MARTY PARKS

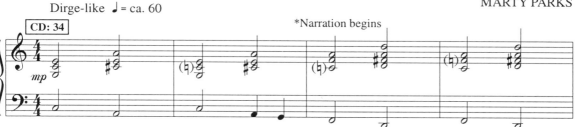

*NARRATOR: For three days the followers of Jesus mourned His loss. Frightened and confused, they must have felt as if they were all a part of some cruel dream. Had Jesus'

ministry been a hoax? Were His words of wisdom and promise all lies? Their hopes had been dashed. Their world had been torn apart. His friends could only stand by and wonder

how their Master, the One they believed to be the Lord of Life, could now lay silent in a cold, dark tomb.

Celebrate the Risen Lord

Christ the Lord Is Risen Today
Rejoice, the Lord Is King
Jesus Shall Reign

Arranged by Marty Parks

NARRATOR *(without music)*: But death could not hold Him, and the grave could not contain Him. *(music begins)* Early in the morning of the third day, love's redeeming work changed

songs of sadness to outbursts of joy. The bleakness of death gave way to the miracle of life. He had risen!

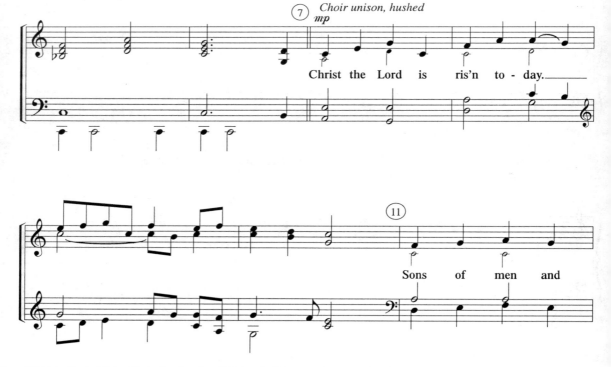

38

40

*"Jesus Shall Reign"

*Words by Isaac Watts; Music by John Hatton. Arr. © 1998 by PsalmSinger Music (BMI). All rights reserved. Administered by The Copyright Company, 40 Music Square East, Nashville, TN 37203.

Who Do You Say I Am?

Underscore

MARTY PARKS

NARRATOR *(without music)*: The good news of the gospel – the death and resurrection of Jesus Christ – is more than just historical fact. This powerful reality still changes lives today. *(music begins)*

Once, before His crucifixion, Jesus asked His disciples, "Who do men say that I am?" They replied, "Some say John the Baptist; others say Elijah; and still others, Jeremiah or one of the prophets."

"But what about you?" He asked. "Who do you say I am?"

Simon Peter answered, "You are the Christ, the Son of the living God."
Christ went on to say that He would build His Church on this one, great

truth and the gates of hell itself would not be able to stand against it.

*And for all of us that question still remains. One by one we must hear
and answer the words of Jesus, the Son of Man: "Who do you say I am?"

You Are the Christ

Solo

Words and Music by
CHERYL SALEM
Arranged by Marty Parks

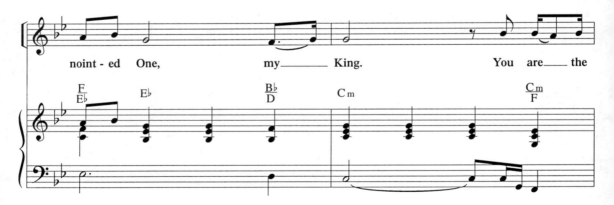

48

Jesus Christ Is Lord

Finale

Words and Music by
MARTY PARKS
Arranged by Marty Parks

*NARRATOR: Listen! The echo of a timeless theme is heard throughout all the earth.
Before anything was created and to this very day, you can hear it. In simple gatherings

and in grand cathedrals, the majestic hymn of angels and millions of blood-bought saints
resounds with this unshakable statement of faith: Jesus Christ is Lord!

50

JESUS

CHRIST

IS

LORD

*An Easter Celebration
of Worship and Praise*

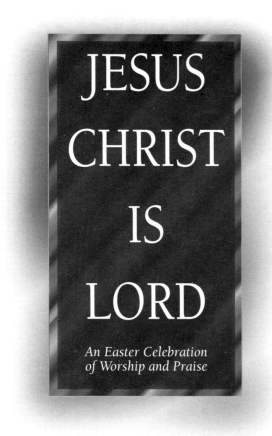